MIRANDA J. GREEN, PhD, FSA

THE GODS OF
ROMAN BRITAIN

SHIRE ARCHAEOLOGY

Cover illustration
Relief from Cirencester depicting the *Deae Matres*
bearing fruit and loaves in their laps.
(Photograph and copyright: Judges Ltd.)

Published by
SHIRE PUBLICATIONS LTD
Cromwell House, Church Street, Princes Risborough,
Aylesbury, Bucks, HP17 9AJ, UK.

Series Editor: James Dyer

ISBN 0 85263 634 2

First published 1983

Set in 11 point Times and printed in Great Britain by
C. I. Thomas & Sons (Haverfordwest) Ltd,
Press Buildings, Merlins Bridge, Haverfordwest, Dyfed.

Contents

LIST OF ILLUSTRATIONS 4

ACKNOWLEDGEMENTS 5

1. THE BEGINNINGS OF ROMANO-BRITISH RELIGION 7

2. PAGAN EASTERN DEITIES 17

3. THE GODS OF ROME 29

4. ROMANO-CELTIC CULTS 43

5. THE CELTIC GODS 51

6. CHRISTIANITY 67

7. MUSEUMS 72

8. SELECT BIBLIOGRAPHY 73

9. GLOSSARY 74

INDEX 75

4

List of illustrations

Plate 1. Bronze boar; Lexden, Essex *page 9*
Plate 2. Bronze bull; Lexden, Essex *page 9*
Plate 3. Model axes; Woodeaton, Oxfordshire *page 12*
Plate 4. Model spears; Woodeaton, Oxfordshire *page 13*
Plate 5. Bronze Mercury; *Verulamium*, Hertfordshire *page 14*
Plate 6. Bronze plaque of anonymous Celtic deity; Woodeaton, Oxfordshire *page 15*
Plate 7. Altar to Mars Lenus Ocelus Vellaunus; Caerwent, Gwent *page 16*
Plate 8. Bull-slaying relief; London, Walbrook *mithraeum page 18*
Plate 9. Marble head of Sarapis; London, Walbrook *mithraeum page 19*
Plate 10. Egg-birth of Mithras; Housesteads, Northumberland *page 21*
Plate 11. Pottery jug with graffito mentioning Isis; London *page 24*
Plate 12. Potsherd depicting Dolichenus; Sawtry, Cambridgeshire *page 27*
Plate 13. Bronze plaque depicting Minerva; Charlton Down, Wiltshire *page 30*
Plate 14. Stone carving of Mars; Bisley, Gloucestershire *page 30*
Plate 15. Bronze plaque depicting Mars; Woodeaton, Oxfordshire *page 32*
Plate 16. Silver plaques to Cocidius; Bewcastle, Cumbria *page 33*
Plate 17. Bronze Mercury; St Donat's, South Glamorgan *page 34*
Plate 18. Marble cockerel; Bancroft Roman villa, Buckinghamshire *page 34*
Plate 19. Stone relief of Vulcan; Duns Tew, Oxfordshire *page 35*
Plate 20. Stone *genius loci;* Carlisle, Cumbria *page 36*
Plate 21. Bronze stag; Colchester, Essex *page 37*
Plate 22. Bronze plaque dedicated to Silvanus Callirius; Colchester *page 38*
Plate 23. Bronze Venus; *Verulamium*, Hertfordshire *page 40*
Plate 24. Pipeclay figurine of 'Venus'; London *page 41*
Plate 25. Stone relief of Mercury; Emberton, Buckinghamshire *page 41*
Plate 26. Stone relief of Mercury and Rosmerta; Gloucester *page 42*
Plate 27. Gilt bronze head of Minerva; Bath, Avon *page 44*
Plate 28. Lead curse invoking Sulis Minerva; Bath *page 45*
Plate 29. Relief of triple Mars; Lower Slaughter, Gloucestershire *page 46*
Plate 30. Bronze equestrian Mars; Peterborough, Cambridgeshire *page 47*
Plate 31. Corinthian capital, (?) from Jupiter column, Cirencester *page 48*
Plate 32. Bronze sceptre-terminal; Willingham Fen, Cambridgeshire *page 49*
Plate 33. Carving of *genius*/wheel-god; Netherby, Cumbria *page 49*
Plate 34. Clay antefix depicting wheel-god; Caerleon, Gwent *page 49*
Plate 35. Relief of *Deae Matres;* Cirencester, Gloucestershire *page 52*
Plate 36. Pipeclay figurines of mother-goddesses; London *page 53*
Plate 37. Bronze Epona; Wiltshire *page 54*
Plate 38. Relief of *genii cucullati* with mother-goddess; Daglingworth, Gloucestershire *page 55*
Plate 39. Relief of *genii cucullati;* Cirencester *page 56*
Plate 40. Clay triple-vase; Chester *page 57*
Plate 41. Bronze eagle; Woodeaton, Oxfordshire *page 59*
Plate 42. Bronze plaque of slain boar; Muntham Court, Sussex *page 61*
Plate 43. Pipeclay triple-horned bull; Colchester, Essex *page 61*
Plate 44. Silvered bronze triple-horned bull; Maiden Castle, Dorset *page 62*
Plate 45. Relief of Cernunnos with ram-horned snakes; Cirencester *page 63*
Plate 46. Altar entwined with ram-horned snake; Lypiatt, Gloucestershire *page 64*
Plate 47. Stone severed head; Caerwent, Gwent *page 64*
Plate 48. Clay face-pot; Caerwent, Gwent *page 66*
Plate 49. Hoard of Christian silver; Water Newton, Cambridgeshire *page 69*

Fig. 1. Bronze statuette of Mars; Foss Dyke, Lincolnshire *page 6*
Fig. 2. Wooden images; Dagenham, Greater London, and Ballachulish, Argyll *page 6*
Fig. 3. Chalk figurine of warrior; Wetwang Slack, Humberside *page 6*
Fig. 4. Bronze bull-head mount; York *page 10*
Fig. 5. Image of boar on shield; river Witham, Lincolnshire *page 10*

Fig. 6. Bronze duck; Milber Down, Devon *page 10*
Fig. 7. Bronze head of Atys; Mildenhall, Suffolk *page 22*
Fig. 8. Bronze mask of Heliosarapis; Felmingham Hall, Norfolk *page 25*
Fig. 9. Bronze head of Claudius; river Alde, Suffolk *page 28*
Fig. 10. Bronze bust of Minerva; Woodeaton, Oxfordshire *page 28*
Fig. 11. Silver plaque to Mars Toutatis; Barkway, Hertfordshire *page 32*
Fig. 12. Gilt bronze Hercules; Birdoswald, Cumbria *page 39*
Fig. 13. Bronze plaque of Apollo; Nettleton Shrub, Wiltshire *page 39*
Fig. 14. Bronze figurine of Ceres; Crewelthorpe, Yorkshire *page 39*
Fig. 15. Bronze tip of ceremonial stave; Felmingham Hall, Norfolk *page 50*
Fig. 16. Bronze wheel model; Felmingham Hall, Norfolk *page 50*
Fig. 17. Silver finger-ring dedicated to Sucellus; York *page 58*
Fig. 18. Sheet-bronze sceptre-binding; Farley Heath, Surrey *page 58*
Fig. 19. Stone bust of horned god; Moresby, Cumbria *page 65*
Fig. 20. Bronze bull-horned head; Athelney, Somerset *page 65*
Fig. 21. Christian wall-painting; Lullingstone, Kent *page 68*
Fig. 22. Christian lead 'font'; Icklingham, Suffolk *page 71*

Acknowledgements

I should like to express my gratitude to the following for their help in the preparation of this book: Eunice Aldhouse, John Ferguson, Stephen Green, Glenys Lloyd-Morgan, P. J. Lopeman and Betty Naggar.

Thanks are due to the following museums for providing me with illustrations and for permission to publish them: Buckinghamshire County Museum, Aylesbury; Roman Baths Museum, Bath; University Museum of Archaeology and Anthropology, Cambridge; National Museum of Wales, Cardiff; Carlisle Museum and Art Gallery; Grosvenor Museum, Chester; Corinium Museum, Cirencester; Colchester and Essex Museum; Devizes Museum; Dorset County Museum, Dorchester; Gloucester City Museum; Trustees of the British Museum, London; Museum of London; Milton Keynes Development Corporation; Museum of Antiquities of the University and the Society of Antiquaries of Newcastle upon Tyne; Ashmolean Museum, Oxford; Peterborough City Museum and Art Gallery; Verulamium Museum, St Albans; Stroud District Museum; Worthing Museum and Art Gallery.

Finally, I should like to thank the Open University in Wales for its encouragement, and for granting me research time to complete this book.

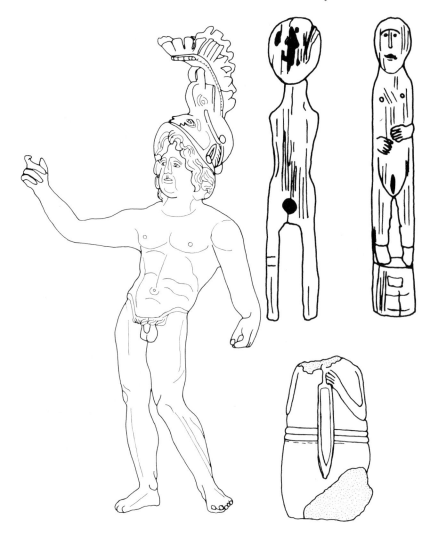

Fig. 1 *(left)*. Hollow-cast bronze statuette of Mars; the figurine is on an inscribed basal plinth (not illustrated), dedicating the figure to Mars and the Spirit of the Emperor. The names of the dedicants are Celtic, that of the craftsman is Roman; Foss Dyke, Lincolnshire. (Illustrator and copyright: Miranda Green.)

Fig. 2 *(top right)*. Wooden figurines representing male and female images, probably of iron age date; left, Dagenham, Greater London; right, Ballachulish, Argyll. (Illustrator and copyright: Miranda Green.)

Fig. 3 *(lower right)*. Chalk figurine of warrior, iron age date; Wetwang Slack, Humberside. (Illustrator and copyright: Miranda Green.)

1
The beginnings of Romano-British religion

Introduction

It is a commonplace, in studies of provincial Roman religion, to state that the nature of the evidence embraces both archaeological and literary material. Nevertheless literary data about Britain are negligible, and the archaeological evidence is much more fragmentary than that from other Celtic provinces. In the study of religion, attempts to answer the question 'what did people believe in?' must be based on evidence for how people expressed their religious beliefs. There are dangers in becoming too speculative and going beyond the limits of the material.

In the Roman period in Britain, there are three major ethnic strands of religion; classical Roman, oriental and native Celtic. The first two existed in the province as a result of their introduction during the Roman occupation. The third strand is indigenous and was already present when the Romans arrived in AD 43. This group of cult material is the most difficult to interpret, since the native Celtic peoples of Britain possessed traditions neither of epigraphy nor of naturalistic representation of divine images. The presence of Rome stimulated the portrayal of gods who, whilst indigenous, were often represented through Roman art forms. The adoption, by Celts, of these classical art media frequently makes it difficult to assess the amount of romanisation — in terms of belief — that is present.

The pre-Roman background

The introduction of Roman culture and religion had a profound effect on that part of the Celtic land of Britain upon which it was superimposed. This may properly be appreciated only by a survey of the evidence for British religion during the five hundred or so years before the Roman occupation. Together with their own religious beliefs and practices, the Romans brought with them the whole classical ethos of depicting human and animal divine images in veristic form (fig. 1), of consistent representation in numerous built sanctuaries, and of using durable materials, such as stone and metal, as vehicles for such images. Whilst in recent years a number of shrines of iron age origin have been identified, images of what may reasonably be interpreted as divine beings are scarce compared with those of the subsequent Romano-British period.

There is a paucity of material evidence for deities in pre-Roman Britain, but the few which do exist are worthy of brief examination. One problem is that secure archaeological contexts are rarely present and whilst an image may look pre-Roman and be Celtic in style it could easily be of Roman date. Some of the crudely carved wooden images, like those from Dagenham (Greater London) and Ballachulish (Argyll) (fig. 2) may date from the iron age. Definitely pre-Roman are the headless chalk figures of warriors from Wetwang Slack (Humberside) (fig. 3). They are probably to be regarded as images of local divinities who had been deliberately and ritually decapitated; perhaps at the time of mutilation they were obsolete as votives and were therefore deconsecrated. The figures were found in the ditch of what may be an iron age ritual enclosure, probably dating between the fourth and first centuries BC.

There is much better evidence for sacred animals in iron age Britain. The bull was a popular Celtic divine beast, frequently represented by its head alone on bucket escutcheons (fig. 4). The boar, too, was important; iron age boar figurines occur in Irish contexts and in Britain appear at, for instance, Hounslow (Greater London) and Woodendean (Sussex), the latter reputedly associated with an early iron age swan's neck pin. The Hounslow boars were found in a field which also produced a bronze miniature wheel, itself perhaps representative of a pre-Roman solar cult. Boar and bull figurines were found together in the immediately pre-Roman Lexden Tumulus outside Colchester (Essex) (plates 1, 2). Boars are of especial interest since they occur constantly on pre-Roman Celtic coinage. They presumably represented strength, ferocity and invincibility in a war-oriented, heroic society such as that of the Celts; this view is endorsed by such occurrences as the boar image on the iron age shield from the river Witham in Lincolnshire (fig. 5). Celtic coinage indicates the presence of other divine beasts, notably the horse, a solar animal in Celtic mythology and frequently accompanied on coins by such solar symbols as spoked wheels. Other animals which occur very occasionally in iron age contexts include aquatic birds, crows and stags, examples of all of which have been discovered at the Milber Down hillfort in Devon (fig. 6).

Apart from human and animal representations, which may represent divinities, worshippers or cult attendants, there is mute

Plate 1. Bronze boar, late iron age; Lexden tumulus, Colchester, Essex. The barrow may have been the burial place of the pre-Roman king Addedomarus. (Photograph and copyright: Colchester and Essex Museum.)

Plate 2. Bronze bull with one knobbed horn (the other is missing), late iron age; Lexden tumulus, Colchester. (Photograph and copyright: Colchester and Essex Museum.)

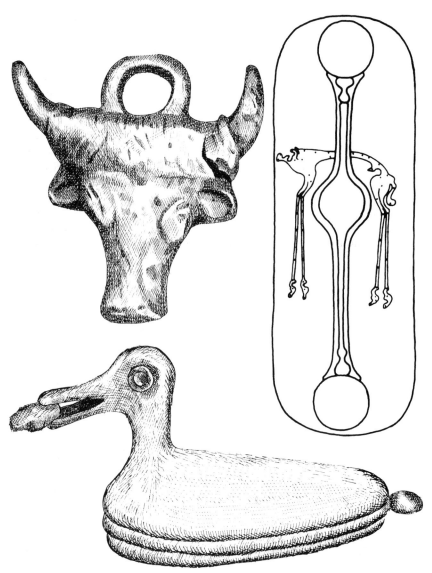

Fig. 4 *(top left)*. Bronze bull-mount; York. (Illustrator: P. J. Lopeman; copyright: Miranda Green.)
Fig. 5 *(top right)*.Outline of shield displaying boar-relief, iron age date; river Witham, Lincolnshire. (Illustrator and copyright: Miranda Green.)
Fig. 6 *(bottom)*. Bronze duck with a cake or pellet in its beak, late iron age date; Milber Down, Devon. (Illustrator: P. J. Lopeman; copyright: Miranda Green.)

evidence of worship in the form of cult deposition. Pre-Roman shrines, like those at Frilford (Oxfordshire) and Worth (Kent), had offerings associated with them in the form of miniature weapons — perhaps dedicated to a warrior-god — and, at Frilford, a ploughshare formed part of a foundation deposit. Miniature weapons and tools recur as offerings during the Roman period (plates 3, 4). The deposition of objects in pits, rivers and lakes was a common practice. At Llyn Cerrig Bach (Anglesey, Gwynedd) tools, weapons and pieces of wheeled vehicles were apparently cast into the lake over a long period. Valuable and undamaged items such as the first-century AD Battersea Shield, which was thrown into the Thames, must surely have been votive offerings.

During the pre-Roman iron age in Britain, there are tantalising glimpses of what must have been a complex set of spiritual beliefs. The most striking aspect of the evidence is not so much its sparseness but its anonymity. Owing to the absence of written sources (including epigraphy) archaeologists can have no idea either of what gods were worshipped nor of the nature of belief. The greatest value of a knowledge of the pre-Roman material lies in being able to evaluate both the amount of innovation in the Roman period and the extent to which the religious practices of the period had their roots in the prehistoric past.

Roman and Celtic religion

The two main ethnic elements in the religion of Roman Britain were Roman (including cults of eastern origin) and Celtic but before the advent of Rome comparatively little evidence for divinities exists. By contrast, classical writers provide abundant information on Roman cults, deities and forms of worship; Rome produced a great deal of iconographical material (based ultimately on Graeco-Roman mythological art) and there was a formalised hierarchy of beliefs and deities classified according to function and based on organised urban society.

In looking at Britain, the need is to assess the process of cultural mixture or collation, produced by Roman conquest and colonisation, and to consider how much the resulting hybrid religion, called 'Romano-Celtic', owed to Roman and how much to Celtic influences. The evidence will, inevitably, produce a picture biased, perhaps unfairly, towards the Roman simply because of the basic Celtic unfamiliarity with naturalistic representation and because allusion to gods by name on inscriptions was a Roman concept foreign to the indigenous population. What

Plate 3. Miniature bronze axes with ritual markings on the blades; Woodeaton Romano-Celtic temple, Oxfordshire. (Photograph: Mrs B. Naggar; copyright: Ashmolean Museum, Oxford.)

the Romans appear to have done is to have provided a catalyst whereby Celtic divine concepts were freed from the bonds of non-representation and anonymity. The use of more or less classical art forms to portray British divinities means that religious entities which would otherwise have remained shrouded in mystery may now for the first time be studied.

The religious iconography of Roman Britain is very varied but most divine images owe something to classical art in the way they are depicted. Graeco-Roman and oriental deities were intro-duced at the time of the conquest and, in many instances, retained their Roman religious form and significance unaltered. At the same time there are native British representations portrayed in a manner almost entirely foreign to classical cultic concepts and art forms except for the fact that they are portrayed at all. In between these two poles there is a wide variety of hybridisation of Roman and Celtic cult images (fig. 1 and caption).

There were differences between Roman and Celtic ways of religious thought. From an examination of iconographical art form alone, it is possible to recognise that in unadulterated form Roman religious evidence is represented in a formalised classical style based largely on Greek prototypes; this style is artistically sound, naturalistic (or idealised) with regard to human or animal form, and easily identifiable by clothing, accompanying attributes or attitude (plate 5). The emblems associated with such images relate either to the character and function of a specific god or to some aspect of his or her mythology. By contrast, portrayals owing little to Roman influence, and which are purely Celtic in style, frequently contain no attributes nor anything positively to identify the figure or its function (plate 6).

Arguing from methods of representation, it is reasonable to deduce that indigenous Celtic religion was at a more primitive stage than that of the Romans. Since there was no organised Celtic state, there could be no universal Celtic state religion (though we know, for instance, from Caesar that there was a Celtic national priesthood, the Druids). Gods in Celtic thought appear not to have been as concerned with functionalistic identity

Plate 4. Miniature bronze spears, ritually bent; Woodeaton Romano-Celtic temple, Oxfordshire. (Photograph: Mrs B. Naggar; copyright: Ashmolean Museum, Oxford.)

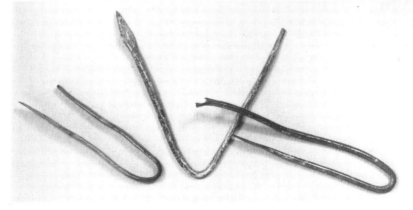

as those of Rome. Local deities with many functions seem to have played a more predominant role in British (and Gaulish) religion than the universal gods of the Olympian pantheon. This may be why the name and art form of the Roman war-god may be used in Celtic lands like Britain but with local, often topographical, surnames attached (plate 7). The significance of the power of Nature and the preoccupations of a rural society are indicated by the prominent role, on the one hand, of beasts and zoomorphic attributes and, on the other, of fertility and prosperity; nearly all deities of Celtic origin may be identified with fecundity and well-being (see chapter 5).

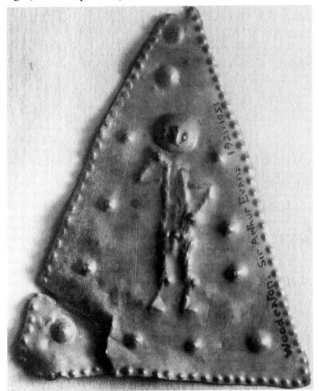

Plate 6 *(above)*. Sheet-bronze plaque of naked, ithyphallic deity with over-large head. The 'matchstick' figure appears to bear an object over his left shoulder; Woodeaton temple, Oxfordshire. (Photograph: Mrs B. Naggar; copyright: Ashmolean Museum, Oxford.)
Plate 5 *(left)*. Bronze Mercury; the god wears a *chlamys* (cloak) and torc; his left hand once held a separately cast *caduceus* now lost. He is accompanied by a cockerel, a ram and a tortoise; *Verulamium*, Hertfordshire. (Photograph and copyright: Verulamium Museum.)

Plate 7. Altar dedicated to Mars Lenus Ocelus Vellaunus and to the Spirit of the Emperor, by Marcus Nonius Romanus. The altar was set up in AD 152; Caerwent, Gwent. (Photograph and copyright: National Museum of Wales, Cardiff.)

2
Pagan eastern deities

Gods and goddesses from all over the oriental world — Asia Minor, Egypt, Persia and Syria — were, by the first century AD, an integral component of the Roman pantheon. The Roman world originally came into contact with eastern culture through conquest and colonisation, through oriental trade and merchants, and through eastern soldiers who made their way into the auxiliary regiments, thus being disseminated all over the Empire.

The oriental mystery religions had a great attraction over cults of Roman origin. Each appears to have involved a personal relationship between an individual and his god. Through processes of secret initiation, merit and good conduct on the part of the devotee, a worshipper could attain happiness in the life to come. This two-way contact between man and god, the idea of striving for perfection and the resulting reward, made oriental religion a live and active mode of devotion, very different from the static, impersonal and stereotyped complex of rituals which the state Roman religion had, to a large extent, become.

Mithraism

Mithras was a Persian god, an emissary of light sent by the great Iranian cosmic deity Ahura Mazda. The mythology of Mithraism is complicated but (and this is a great oversimplification) involved Mithras being sent to earth to hunt and kill a divine bull, the release of whose blood symbolised life-giving forces. It is this bull-slaying scene which is depicted on the *reredos* or main altar stone in *mithraea* (Mithraic temples) (plate 8). Mithraism was a dualistic religion and the evil, negative, dark element played a necessary part. Thus Ahriman, the power of disorder and darkness, is known, and on the tauroctonous (bull-slaying) reliefs seemingly evil forces such as the scorpion and serpent are present, their role being to try to prevent the life-blood reaching and fertilising the earth (plate 8).

A number of small *mithraea* are present in the region of Hadrian's Wall, at for example Carrawburgh and Housesteads, and at *Segontium* (Caernarfon) in north-west Wales. The best known site is the Walbrook *mithraeum* in London. The shrines themselves are of homogeneous type (known as far apart as

Plate 8. Marble relief depicting a Mithraic bull-slaying scene. In the central roundel, Mithras, wearing pointed cap, tunic, cloak and trousers, kneels astride a bull and plunges a dagger into its neck. With the god are Cautes and Cautopates, a dog, snake and scorpion. Encircling the scene are the signs of the zodiac; outside the roundel Sol (upper left) drives his chariot; Luna is on the top right; in the lower corners are busts of wind deities. The relief bears a votive inscription probably reading 'Ulpius Silvanus, veteran of Legion II Augusta, paid his vow: he was initiated at Orange'; Walbrook, *mithraeum*, London. (Photograph and copyright: Museum of London.)

Britain and the eastern Empire), consisting of a sunken nave, giving the semblance of the cave of the original bull-slaying myth, and two raised side-aisles. The ritual (which included seven grades of initiation for worshippers) would have taken place in semi-darkness, with altars and cult reliefs illuminated by torchlight. The British *mithraea* have, between them, yielded a great deal of sculptural material in the form of statues, reliefs and altars. London has produced a number of depictions of Mithras himself (plate 8), but tolerance of other cults is evidenced by high-quality sculptures of Sarapis (plate 9), a river-god, Bacchus, the Dioscuri, Atargatis, Mercury, Minerva and a *Bonus Eventus* (Good Outcome), all dating to the mid-late second century AD. The most important sculpture from

Plate 9. Marble head of Sarapis; on the head is a corn-measure or *modius* (a fertility symbol), decorated with olive-trees; Walbrook *mithraeum*, London. (Photograph and copyright: Museum of London.)

Housesteads is a relief showing one of the mythological tales of
Mithras' origins, his birth from an egg (plate 10), and the carving
shows also the curving vault of the sky and the signs of the
zodiac. The cosmic element in Mithraism is indicated here, as on
several of the tauroctonous reliefs, where zodiacal symbols and
depictions of the sun itself are frequently present (plate 8).
Altars in *mithraea* are commonly dedicated to the 'Unconquered
Sun', the sun being another power of light, and at the entrance
to the shrines stood two Persian-clad figures (Cautes and
Cautopates), one with upright torch, one with torch inverted,
symbolising light and darkness (plate 8). This dark, anti-Mithras
element is evidenced in Britain by a find from Caerwent, where
a statue of Ahriman is recorded, although not from a known
mithraeum. A number of cult objects occur elsewhere in Britain.

The distribution of British *mithraea* is significant — in the main
centres of army activity and in the great commercial centre of
London. We know that Mithraism was an entirely masculine cult,
one which appealed especially to the wealthier echelons of the
Roman army. Merchants also were attracted to the cult and this
may explain the presence of a large, opulent *mithraeum* at
London.

The Anatolian cults

The worship of the great Phrygian mother-goddess Cybele and
her young consort Atys is recorded both in northern and southern
Britain. We do not know as much about the cult as about
Mithraism, but it appears to have centred around a cyclical myth
personified by the castration, death and rebirth of Cybele's
youthful shepherd lover Atys. The goddess caught Atys in
infidelity and drove him mad so that he castrated himself beneath
a pine-tree and bled to death. In the ceremonies a festival of
mourning was followed by a joyous ceremony, the *hilaria,* when
the rebirth of Atys and the new year were celebrated. The rites
involved the *taurobolium* or bull sacrifice, ecstatic dances and, in
some cases, the self-flagellation and castration of initiates to the
priesthood.

The cult of Cybele was introduced to Rome in 205 BC, but
Roman citizens were forbidden to participate in such orgiastic
rituals and could aspire only to membership of supporting guilds.
It was not until the reign of Claudius that bans on participation
were lifted and Romans could become *galli* or priests of Cybele.

In Britain, objects relating to this cult occur typically in the
towns, notably at London, in the *colonia* at Gloucester and in the

Plate 10. Sculpture depicting the birth of Mithras from an egg. The surrounding cosmic vault shows the signs of the zodiac; Mithras' hands can be seen against the frame, one holding a knife, the other a torch; Housesteads Roman fort, Northumberland. (Photograph and copyright: Museum of Antiquities of the University and the Society of Antiquaries of Newcastle upon Tyne.)

area of Hadrian's Wall. London was of particular importance for the cult, as for the other oriental mysteries. In lowland Britain, about forty cult items have been discovered. No traces of *metroons* (shrines for Cybele worship) are recorded but they probably existed in London, Gloucester and Corbridge, where large stone cult objects are recorded. In London an altar to Cybele, now lost, portrayed relief carvings of priests, a mourning procession bearing the dead Atys, pine-cones and cymbals. The city produced also a stone figure of the young Atys and a number of small bronze personal cult objects including traders' steelyard weights in the form of Cybele and a fine figurine of Atys from the Thames. Perhaps the most curious London item is a serrated bronze 'clamp' decorated with busts of the two Anatolian deities and zoomorphic attendants. Finds from Gloucester imply at least one temple. Two sculptures depict Atys; one portrays the god as a child wearing the soft pointed Phrygian cap; the other consists

Fig. 7. Bronze head of Atys, wearing soft pointed *pileus* or Phrygian cap; Mildenhall, Suffolk. (Illustrator: P. J. Lopeman; copyright: Miranda Green.)

of an altar to Atys, depicting a young god wearing the pointed cap and accompanied by a bag and *syrinx* (pipes). Elsewhere in southern Britain, shrines are suggested by a fragmentary torso of Atys from a villa at Froxfield (Wiltshire) and by a mosaic depicting Cybele at the Whatley Roman villa (Somerset); these two finds are of interest in their suggestion of the possible presence of private house shrines. The evidence from Hockwold (Norfolk) is of great importance; the presence here, at a rural East Anglian temple, of a bronze jug depicting the head of Atys on the handle shows the extent of penetration to relatively unromanised parts of Britain of cult items representing this sophisticated oriental religion. At Mildenhall (Suffolk) in the same tribal area (that of the Iceni), a small bronze head of Atys is recorded (fig. 7).

In northern Britain, the main centre for the cult of the Great Mother appears to have been at Corbridge, where a fine altar and a worn head attest corporate worship. A small pipeclay figurine of Cybele from the site represents the offering of a poorer individual devotee.

The Egyptian pantheon

Isis, originally a moon and fertility goddess, Sarapis (god of sky and death) and Harpocrates, their son, follow the pattern of other eastern deities in Britain in being represented most commonly in the towns. Sarapis and Harpocrates are Graeco-Roman versions of the ancient Egyptian gods Osiris and Horus. At Rome itself, political problems with Egypt at the end of the Republic discouraged the acceptance of these divinities, but Gaius and his successors actively encouraged the worship of the Egyptian pantheon and these divinities were introduced to Britain at the time of the occupation. The cult of Isis was a mystery religion involving initiation, baptism, service and eventual salvation. The underlying mythology involves death and rebirth; Osiris somehow overcame death, and in the same way, by baptism, initiates could be reborn. Sarapis possessed sky, healing and underworld functions.

In Britain, temples to both Isis and Sarapis are recorded. At York a shrine to the holy god Sarapis was dedicated by Claudius Hieronymianus of the VI Legion. In London an *isaeum* (shrine to Isis) is implied by the presence of a jug scratched with the graffito *Londini ad fanum Isidis* (plate 11) and by a third-century AD stone inscription.The processions of priests carrying *sistra* (tinkling rattles) are evidenced by iron models of *sistra* from London

Plate 11. Clay flagon bearing the legend *Londini ad fanum Isidis;* London. (Photograph and copyright: Museum of London.)

Fig. 8. Bronze mask of Heliosarapis, with radiate solar headdress; Felmingham Hall, Norfolk. (Illustrator: P. J. Lopeman; copyright: Miranda Green.)

and by a bronze full-size rattle from Exeter. Sarapis is represented by a fine marble head found at the London *mithraeum* (plate 9); by another in porphyry from a grave at Highworth (Wiltshire); and by a stone head, probably of Antonine origin, from Silchester. A personal cult object in the form of a bronze ring decorated with a head of Sarapis comes from Stone (Buckinghamshire); steelyard weights depicting Isis come from London; a statuette depicting the goddess is recorded from Dorchester (Dorset); and more significant is a figurine from the vicinity of the Romano-Celtic temple precinct at Thornborough (Buckinghamshire).

Portrayals of Harpocrates (the Egyptian sky-god Horus becomes in Graeco-Roman contexts a *genius* or spirit of watchfulness, self-nourishment and silence) occur as statuettes mainly in London. The finest of these is a silver-washed bronze and represents the god with wings, lunar crescent, dog, tortoise and snake. The figure is naked and adopts the characteristic pose of the index finger of one hand touching the mouth (symbolic of quiet or self-nourishment or both). It was obviously a valued item since, in addition to the silvering, a gold chain is slung diagonally across the body.

Obscurer Egyptian deities occur occasionally in Britain. Horus, depicted as a falcon in original Egyptian form, is evidenced by a small figurine from a shrine at Farley Heath (Surrey). Thoth, the god of medicine and wisdom, is represented by bronze ibis heads from Chiddingfold villa (Surrey) and from Caerwent (Gwent). Jupiter-Ammon occurs in Kent; Heliosarapis (a fusion of Sarapis with the Greek sun-god) in Norfolk (fig. 8); Bes (a fertility godling) and the Apis Bull of Osiris are each represented.

The divinities of Syria

Syrian deities may simply be divided into sky and weather gods or Baals and goddesses (Astarte or Atargatis). There was no universal pantheon in Syria; in its place there existed local, omnipotent city-deities who sometimes attained wider status and were exported to Rome and thence to the western provinces. The most important Baal introduced to Britain was Jupiter Dolichenus, the result of the fusion of the identities of Jupiter and the local weather and iron god of Doliche at Commagene. No Syrian divinities are well represented on British sites but Dolichenus is perhaps the most common, being present at Corbridge in the region of Hadrian's Wall. Virtually all Dolichene material comes from parts of Britain with an important military presence; the distribution tends to correlate with military-worked iron ore deposits, and the god may appear here in his capacity as presider over iron-producing activities. The very much scarcer southern British material includes a Castor-ware sherd representing the god with his conical cap and brandishing his double-axe (probably a thunderbolt symbol) from Sawtry (Cambridgeshire) (plate 12) and a bronze head of the god from Cirencester (Gloucestershire).

The enigmatic cult of Astarte and Hercules of Tyre is represented by two Greek-inscribed altars, designed as a pair, at Corbridge. The great Syrian Mother, Atargatis (or *Dea Syria),* whose fertility emblem was the fish, is known both in northern Britain and at London, in the Walbrook *mithraeum.*

Finally we should make mention of *Sol Invictus* (the Unconquered Sun). The Emperor Aurelian in the mid third century AD established the Sun as a supreme Roman Deity. Aurelian was

Plate 12. Sherd of Castor ware depicting Jupiter Dolichenus with conical cap and double-axe; Sawtry, Cambridgeshire. (Photograph and copyright: Peterborough City Museum and Art Gallery.)

thoroughly involved with Syria and the Syrian army and the main god of Palmyra was *Sol Invictus.* The god is represented in Corbridge, London and in several *mithraea.*

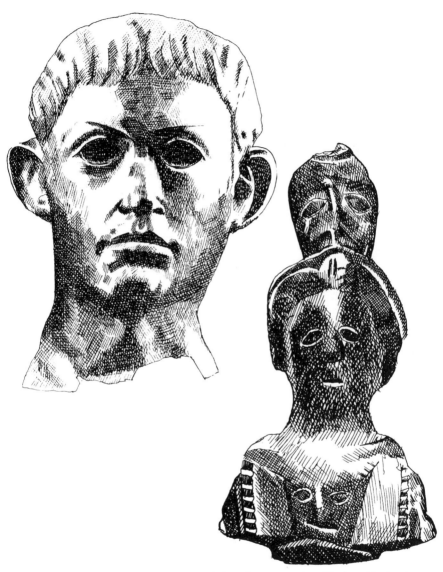

Fig. 9 *(left)*. Hollow-cast bronze head of Claudius; larger than life-size. The head was probably deliberately hacked from the body during the time of the Boudiccan revolt (AD 61); river Alde, Rendham, Suffolk. (Illustrator: P. J. Lopeman; copyright: Miranda Green.)
Fig. 10 *(right)*. Bronze bust of Minerva; Woodeaton Roman temple-site, Oxfordshire. (Illustrator: P. J. Lopeman; copyright: Miranda Green.)

3
The gods of Rome

The substantial degree of fusion and interaction between Roman and native cults in Roman Britain was discussed in chapter 1, and further examples of this will be described below (chapter 4). In this chapter the major divinities introduced from Rome to Britain are examined and their Roman aspect analysed, regardless of whether, in some instances, they became mingled with Celtic cult concepts.

The Imperial cult
The cult of the Spirit of Rome and the Emperor naturally had no pre-Roman precedent. The most important evidence for the Imperial cult in Britain is the temple of Claudius at Colchester, recorded by both literary evidence (Tacitus and Seneca) and archaeological sources. This temple may not have been completed until the early part of Vespasian's reign and was probably not dedicated until after Claudius' death. Other British material indicates the presence of the cult of the Emperor. Large bronze images of Claudius, perhaps from Colchester but found in the river Alde (fig. 9), and of Hadrian in London are recorded. Priests of the cult are attested at Lincoln and York. A number of altars both from north and south Britain were dedicated to the *Numen* or Spirit of the Emperor, sometimes linked with other divinities. At Colchester the Imperial cult was linked with the obscure Celtic cult of Mercury Andescocioucus.

The Capitoline triad
The three major state gods of Rome were Jupiter, Juno and Minerva. Jupiter was essentially a sky divinity, but he possessed the additional role of being both the head of the Roman pantheon and, as Jupiter Best and Greatest, representative of the spirit of Rome itself. Juno as his consort shared his dominance over other deities and was, in addition, the main goddess of women and femininity. Minerva was a goddess of war, wisdom and crafts.

As far as iconography is concerned, Juno is of least significance in the province; she occurs relatively infrequently but is repre-

Plate 13 *(left)*. Bronze plaque depicting Minerva; Charlton Down, Wiltshire. (Photograph and copyright: Devizes Museum.)
Plate 14 *(right)*. Relief of Mars with spear and shield; Bisley, Gloucestershire. (Photograph and copyright: Stroud District Museum.)

sented on small figurines, for example in London, Chester and possibly at York. Juno's sky emblem, the peacock, is portrayed on small bronzes from London, York and Corbridge. Minerva is of more interest in that she appears not only in unadulterated Roman form but also in Celtic guise. The goddess in normal classical form occurs on fine, probably imported, bronzes from Canterbury and Plaxtol in Kent and elsewhere (fig. 10). The style and body proportions of a sculpture from Lypiatt Park (Gloucestershire) indicate Celtic workmanship but there is no indication that the goddess is other than the Roman deity. The bronze plaque depicting Minerva from Charlton Down (Wiltshire) (plate 13) likewise demonstrates a certain degree of non-realism. But it is at Bath that Minerva shows herself fully equated with a Celtic goddess, Sulis; we shall return to Sulis-Minerva in chapter 4.

The cult of Jupiter Optimus Maximus (Jupiter Best and Greatest) would have been introduced to conquered provinces more as a focus of loyalty and fealty to Rome than as an individual personal god. Representations of Jupiter, like those of Minerva, exhibit a degree of celticism, but it is as a purely Roman god that we now examine evidence for his cult. Forts like Birdoswald and Maryport in Cumbria, on or near Hadrian's Wall, have each produced some twenty altars set up to *Iuppiter Optimus Maximus* and it is probable that these altars represent the annual renewal of allegiance by Roman troops who each year, on 3rd January, buried the old altar and set up a new one in its place. In bronze there occur well made, naturalistic images in Graeco-Roman style. A seated bronze Jupiter comes from West Stoke in Sussex, and others are recorded in urban contexts such as London.

Mars and Mercury

Both Mars and Mercury were particularly popular in both Britain and Gaul. Like Jupiter and Minerva, each underwent substantial Celtic influence, but it is as Roman introductions to the province that we assess them here.

Mars, as a classical god of war, occurs commonly, as one would expect, in the areas of Britain which had a permanent military presence, namely the north and west. Many dedications on stone survive from northern forts, as at Benwell and Housesteads, but few small bronzes are recorded from the frontier areas. It is curious that southern Britain, where military occupation was relatively brief and transitory, has produced a great deal of evidence for the cult of Mars (plate 14). Barkway (Hertfordshire) (fig. 11) and Stony Stratford (Buckinghamshire) have each produced hoards of ritual silver, including plaques depicting and dedicated to both classical and Celtic versions of Mars. A similar plaque in bronze comes from the temple site at Woodeaton (Oxfordshire) (plate 15), and the model spears from the same site may also have been offerings to the warrior-god (plate 4). Bronze figurines of classical type come from, for example, Bury St Edmunds (Suffolk), Foss Dyke (Lincolnshire) (fig. 1) and Earith (Cambridgeshire). Some stone depictions of Mars betray Celtic influence in style, but not necessarily in terms of religion. Thus some of the Cotswold altars (e.g. plate 14) may represent a classical rather than a Celtic Mars. Very stylised portrayals, like a recently discovered relief from Newtown (Powys), must have

Fig. 11. Silver plaque dedicated to Mars Toutatis, from ritual hoard; Barkway, Hertfordshire. (Illustrator and copyright: Miranda Green.)

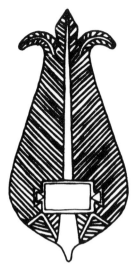

Plate 15. Sheet-bronze plaque decorated with figure of Mars in repoussé. The god wears tunic, cuirass, cloak, boots and crested helmet; he carries a spear and shield; Woodeaton temple, Oxfordshire. (Photograph: Mrs B. Naggar; copyright: Ashmolean Museum, Oxford.)

Plate 16. Two silver plaques dedicated to the Celtic god Cocidius; both show a stylised warrior deity and, on the larger, a shield and spear may be seen; Bewcastle, Cumbria. (Photograph and copyright: Carlisle Museum and Art Gallery.)

been intended for a Celtic worshipper. The style, executed in a similar 'shorthand' or schematic manner to that of the Mars-Cocidius plaques from Bewcastle (plate 16) (see chapter 4), would neither have been recognisable to nor appreciated by Roman or romanised devotees.

Mercury is the best represented divinity in Britain, reflecting Gaulish traditions. Like Mars, he lent himself to a wide variety of celticism, but he occurs in his classical role as a messenger and, more importantly, as a trader-god throughout the province. In the lowland regions over fifty small figurines of the god are recorded, mostly in bronze, and about a dozen or more from northern and western regions. One may cite, for instance, the bronze from St Donat's in south-east Wales (plate 17) and an elaborate bronze from *Verulamium* (Hertfordshire) (plate 5). On this bronze, Mercury wears a silver torc (a Celtic necklet) and he is here associated with his cockerel (herald of the new day, reflecting Mercury's role as herald of the gods), a tortoise (a

Plate 17 *(left).* Bronze Mercury with *petasos* (winged hat), purse and *chlamys;* St Donat's, South Glamorgan. (Photograph and copyright: National Museum of Wales, Cardiff.)
Plate 18 *(right).* Carrara marble cockerel, probably from Mercury group of later second-century date; Bancroft Roman villa, Buckinghamshire. (Photograph and copyright: Milton Keynes Development Corporation.)

reference to Mercury's invention of the lyre from a tortoise-shell) and a ram (a fertility symbol). Fine stone representations include the seated Mercury of marble from the Walbrook *mithraeum,* and the Cirencester relief showing the naked god standing with his winged hat, *caduceus* and accompanying cockerel. The Bancroft Roman villa has produced a cockerel of Carrara marble, probably from a Mercury group (plate 18). The most significant recent discovery associated with the cult of Mercury is the temple site at Uley (Gloucestershire). British temples rarely yield positive identification as to dedication but here the major cult definitely seems to have been that of Mercury. Finds include part of a deliberately mutilated cult statue of the god in very classical style and probably of mid second-century date, two fragmentary reliefs of Mercury with goat and cockerel, and a number of bronze figurines. Other features of special interest include the presence of several hundred lead curses *(defixiones)* invoking Mercury, and the occurrence of over 230,000 animal bones, the most frequent being those of goat or sheep and fowl (Mercury's two most important zoomorphic attendants). There is evidence of religious activity on the site of Uley from prehistory to the sixth century AD; the stone shrine to Mercury appears to have been erected in the second century AD.

Plate 19. Stone relief of the smith-god Vulcan. The figure is worn but hammer, tongs and anvil may be seen; Duns Tew, Oxfordshire. (Photograph and copyright: Ashmolean Museum, Oxford.)

Plate 20. Stone *genius loci*. The stylised, semi-draped figure wears a mural crown and holds a cornucopiae and a *patera* over an altar; Carlisle. (Photograph and copyright: Carlisle Museum and Art Gallery.)

Plate 21. Bronze stag, found in a pit in the vicinity of a rectangular temple, in association with an inscribed plaque (plate 22); Colchester. (Photograph and copyright: Colchester and Essex Museum.)

Other classical gods and goddesses

Almost every classical deity familiar to the Roman world is represented in Britain in some form. The most popular gods include the demigod Hercules, Silvanus, Vulcan (plate 19) and *Genii* (plate 20). Hercules appears to retain his Roman character virtually intact. A representation of the god occurs with his club and wine-cup on a corner-stone of the great Bath altar, and a large gilded bronze from Birdoswald (fig. 12) is another example of the cult. The woodland god Silvanus was a rustic divinity who would have fitted well into a Celtic rural context. Sometimes, as at the temple of Nettleton Shrub (Wiltshire), he is associated epigraphically with the Spirit of the Emperor. Silvanus himself is rarely definitely identifiable as a human depiction, though native hunter-gods are common and may represent crude indigenous versions of Silvanus. But Silvanus' favourite zoomorphic companion, the stag, occurs more frequently, as at Colchester, where a stag figurine was found in a pit associated with a shrine and with a dedication to Silvanus (plates 21, 22). Apollo, the classical god of healing, prophecy and — later — of the sun was not especially common in Britain, but at Nettleton Shrub in Wiltshire a shrine

Plate 22. Bronze plaque bearing punched dedication to Silvanus Callirius, by a coppersmith. Found with stag (plate 21). (Photograph and copyright: Colchester and Essex Museum.)

was dedicated to the god (fig. 13). *Genii* (spirits of places and other concepts) are common as stone carvings (plate 20). *Genii loci* represent the spirit of a given place and embody concepts of protection and well-being. They are distinguished iconographically by their bearing of a *cornucopiae* crooked against one shoulder, with a *patera* (offering plate) held over an altar by the other hand. They may, like the badly proportioned little figure from Carlisle (plate 20), wear a turreted mural crown, symbolising their suzerainty over a town. Other classical gods who occur more or less commonly include Aesculapius (a healer), Bacchus, Cupid and Neptune.

Of the goddesses, apart from Juno and Minerva, those represented include Venus (plate 23), Fortuna, Victory, Diana, Ceres (a corn-goddess) (fig. 14), Luna, Flora and Vesta (keeper of the hearth and fire). Of these only the first four occur with any frequency. Venus usually occurs either as a small bronze figure, like the second-century *Verulamium* example (plate 23), or as a white pipeclay statuette (plate 24). The clay figures, however, represent an essentially Celtic divine concept (see chapter 5). Diana, the Huntress, occurs both in bronze and on stone reliefs. A marble fragment of Diana comes from a shrine at Maiden Castle; also from a temple, at Nettleton Shrub, comes a relief of

Fig. 12 *(left).* Large gilt bronze figurine of Hercules, wearing Nemaean lionskin; Birdoswald, Cumbria. (Illustrator: P. J. Lopeman; copyright: Miranda Green.)

Fig. 13 *(top right).* Bronze plaque dedicated to Apollo. The plaque, dedicated by one Decimus, was found on the floor of an improvised shrine probably used during the later fourth century AD; Nettleton Shrub, Wiltshire. (Illustrator and copyright: Miranda Green.)

Fig. 14 *(lower right).* Bronze figurine of Ceres; Crewelthorpe, Yorkshire. (Illustrator: P. J. Lopeman; copyright: Miranda Green.)

Plate 23. Bronze Venus, holding fruit in her left hand; second-century date; *Verulamium*, Hertfordshire. (Photograph and copyright: Verulamium Museum.)

Diana and her hound. At the great therapeutic spring sanctuary at Bath an altar to Diana was dedicated by a freedman, Vettius Benignus. Fortuna and Victory were divinities especially beloved of soldiers and as such are particularly common in the region of Hadrian's Wall. The reason for Victory's popularity in this context is self-evident, but Fortuna (Chance) was invoked especially in bath-houses where soldiers were naked and vulner-

Plate 24 *(left)*. White pipeclay (china clay) figurine of goddess resembling Venus; London. (Photograph and copyright: Museum of London.)
Plate 25 *(right)*. Stone Mercury relief; the stylised figure is winged (or horned), wears a pleated knee-length tunic and bears a *caduceus* in the left hand. From a pit at Emberton, Buckinghamshire. (Photograph and copyright: Buckinghamshire County Museum.)

able. Chance and Victory are just two examples of female personifications of abstract ideas; others include Discipulina (especially relevant to soldiers), Salus (Health) and Nemesis (Revenge).

Faunus

A recent discovery relating to Roman gods in Britain is of great importance in that it provides the only evidence for the cult of Faunus in the province; he is rarely attested archaeologically anywhere. A hoard of late fourth-century jewellery and silver plate, discovered at Thetford (Norfolk), is composed of gold and silver objects and other precious items. The significance for ritual lies in the presence of silver spoons dedicated to the rural Italian deity Faunus. It is curious to find such a denizen of the Italian countryside in East Anglia, and the discovery is made even more interesting by the association of Faunus with obscure Celtic spirits, unknown outside this hoard.

Plate 26. Relief of Mercury and Rosmerta. Mercury wears a *chlamys* and is winged; he bears a purse and *caduceus*, beside which is a cock. Rosmerta bears a long-shafted object in one hand and a *patera* held over an altar in the other; Gloucester. (Photograph and copyright: Gloucester City Museum.)

4
Romano-Celtic cults

Certain Roman deities in Britain were subjected to substantial Celtic influence, whilst still retaining their Roman identity. This hybridisation took a number of forms. The style of some depictions, like the stone Mercury from Emberton (Buckinghamshire) (plate 25), may betray nothing more than bad art but owes so little to verism that it is doubtful whether such a cult object would appeal to a Roman or romanised worshipper. Mercury undergoes other forms of celticism in his association with a non-classical Celtic consort, Rosmerta (plate 26), and at, for instance, Chesters and Uley, where he is horned. Roman gods may possess Celtic surnames, like Silvanus Callirius (Woodland King) at Colchester (plate 22) and Apollo Cunomaglus (Hound Lord) at Nettleton. Deities with Roman attributes may be associated also with non-Roman iconographical features or contexts, which may reflect identification with pre-existing Celtic gods. Whilst it is impossible to consider here all Roman deities displaying celticism, three divinities stand out as being of major significance in this context, namely Sulis Minerva, the Celtic Mars and a Romano-Celtic sky-god.

Sulis Minerva
Minerva's identification with a Celtic goddess may be exemplified by one site, the healing cult establishment at Bath. Here, in terms of physical appearance (plate 27), Minerva could be wholly classical. The over life-size gilded bronze head is completely Graeco-Roman in style. But we know from epigraphic evidence — from stone altars and lead curses (plate 28) — that the goddess worshipped at Bath was Sulis Minerva. Sulis was a Celtic goddess already present before the Roman period, probably as a healing power. When the Romans exploited the therapeutic potential of the thermal spring, Sulis became equated with Minerva. Recent excavations in the Roman reservoir at Bath have recovered new evidence for the cult. A great number of lead curses (plate 28) attest the invocation of Sulis Minerva, and over six thousand coins were cast as offerings into the water.

The Celtic Mars
The Roman god of war appears in Britain in a number of

Plate 27. Larger than life-size gilt bronze head of Minerva; Bath, Avon. (Photograph and copyright: Roman Baths Museum, Bath.)

different forms or guises. We have seen that he has a conventional warrior role, where he appears more or less in authentic Graeco-Roman form (fig. 1, plate 14). Mars is of interest, however, for two main reasons. First, under Celtic influence, he is frequently depicted with crude simplicity, as a kind of 'matchstick man' (plate 16). Second, he is identified epigraphically with a number of Celtic entities. Some of these, like Mars Cocidius (plate 16) or Belatucadrus in north Britain, adhere to the traditional war role; but in other, especially southern contexts, Mars is transformed both epigraphically and artistically and assumes a peaceful function. At Caerwent, Mars is called Lenus Ocelus Vallaunus (plate 7), perhaps a healing god, as we know that a healing cult of Mars Lenus existed at Trier in

Plate 28. Lead *defixio* (curse) invoking Sulis Minerva; Roman reservoir, Bath. (Photograph and copyright: Roman Baths Museum, Bath.)

Germany. In Gloucestershire, at Bisley and Custom Scrubs, Mars is portrayed armed but with a *cornucopiae* a symbol of plenty and of bucolic well-being. At Lower Slaughter (Gloucestershire) Mars occurs in triplicate, indicating Celtic influence in the apparent potency of the number three (plate 29). The other transformation Mars undergoes is mainly localised to eastern Britain, but with outliers elsewhere. This is the depiction of a warrior-god on horseback (plate 30), an unfamiliar classical method of Mars imagery. A temple complex dedicated to a warrior horseman existed at Brigstock (Northamptonshire), but one of the best preserved representations is the bronze figurine from Peterborough (Cambridgeshire) (plate 30). At Martlesham (Suffolk) a statuette of a mounted warrior is associated with an inscription dedicating the bronze to Mars Corotiacus; thus we have indirect evidence that Mars is probably being portrayed on the other, anonymous, bronzes described above.

The Romano-Celtic sky-god

Whilst the Roman sky-god, Jupiter, is prominent in Britain, there is evidence both for celticisation of the Roman god and for the separate existence of a Celtic sky divinity, specifically solar, identified, to some extent, with the Roman god. Epigraphically the only evidence for a Romano-Celtic Jupiter is a worn altar from Chester dedicated to Jupiter Optimus Maximus Tanarus, the last word referring to a Celtic thunder deity known archaeologically in Gaul and Germany, and mentioned also by the Roman poet Lucan. The Romano-Celtic sky-god occurs iconographically in two main forms. The first is demonstrated by the existence of Jupiter columns. No complete examples of these survive in Britain, where they are few in number and where the most important part, the sculptured summit group, is not present. Jupiter columns are a type of monument confined mainly to

Plate 29. Stone relief of triple Mars, each with sword and shield; from a well at Lower Slaughter, Gloucestershire. (Photograph and copyright: Gloucester City Museum.)

Plate 30. Bronze horseman-god, wearing a cloak and Corinthian helmet, and bearing the shield of an auxiliary. The group stands on a convex baseplate. (Photograph and copyright: Peterborough City Museum and Art Gallery.)

north-east Gaul and Germany. When complete, they consist of superimposed four- and eight-sided stone bases carved with deities and with a dedication to Jupiter; above rises a high column, often ornamented to symbolise a tree; above again is a figured Corinthian capital and at the summit stands a carved group most commonly representing a horseman riding down (or being supported by) a monster with snake limbs. This is usually interpreted as an allegory or dualistic myth concerning the conflict between light and darkness, good and evil, life and death. The dedication is to Jupiter, but the classical god never appears on horseback and it is probable that a Celtic sky cult is here represented under the guise of a Roman god. The most likely British candidate for such a monument comes from Cirencester, where a large figured capital survives (plate 31), together with an inscribed stone mentioning the restoration of a statue and column in honour of Jupiter.

The second Romano-Celtic manifestation of Jupiter, more important for Britain, is his identification with a Celtic solar god

Plate 31. Figured Corinthian capital, perhaps from a Jupiter column; the capital is carved with the busts of beings associated with Bacchic ritual; Cirencester, Gloucestershire. (Photograph: C. J. Bowler; copyright: Corinium Museum.)

Plate 32 *(left)*. Bronze sceptre-terminal depicting a young god accompanied by an eagle, wheel, dolphin and triple-horned bull's head, and resting his foot on the head of an anthropomorphic being. The god bears a club or thunderbolt in his left hand; Willingham Fen, Cambridgeshire. (Photograph and copyright: Cambridge University Museum of Archaeology and Anthropology.)

Plate 33 *(top right)*. Relief of headless *Genius* or *Bonus Eventus*. The left arm once supported a cornucopia; the right holds a large eight-spoked wheel over a small altar; Netherby. (Photograph and copyright: Carlisle Museum and Art Gallery.)

Plate 34 *(lower right)*. Clay antefix with an eight-spoked wheel above a human head, and with flanking star symbols; Caerleon legionary fortress, Gwent. (Photograph and copyright: National Museum of Wales, Cardiff.)

whose main symbol was the spoked wheel. This object is not normally associated with the Roman Jupiter but occurs on altars in north Britain, as at Birdoswald and Castlesteads, which are inscribed with usual military Roman dedications to Jupiter. The Celtic solar god is represented also on cult items not overtly connected with Jupiter. Perhaps the most complex of these in terms of iconographic detail is a bronze sceptre-terminal from Willingham Fen (Cambridgeshire) (plate 32). Depicted here is a youthful, naked god resting his foot on the head of a being disappearing into the earth (recalling the imagery of Jupiter columns). The god is accompanied by an eagle (emblem of Jupiter), a solar wheel, a dolphin and a triple-horned bull's head. The imagery here is obscure but the wheel and eagle at least would appear to be celestial symbols. The trampled being could be chthonic, and the dolphin too may be a death symbol (it has this significance in the classical world). At Corbridge a wheel-bearing figure appears on a clay mould represented as a warrior armed with shield and club, possibly again symbols of the battle of a light-god against darkness and death. At Netherby (Cumbria) (plate 33) the Celtic solar god appears in the manner of a classical *Bonus Eventus* (or good luck personification) with the *cornucopiae* of prosperity and a wheel (instead of the usual *patera*) held over an altar. At Caerleon (Gwent) the solar deity seems to owe very little to classicism, and no connection with Jupiter is apparent. Here, at a legionary fortress, clay antefixes (triangular tiles affixed to the gable-ends of roofs) portray solar wheels and moon and star images associated with human heads — presumably representing the solar god himself (plate 34). One final occurrence of interest is the hoard of religious bronzes from Felmingham Hall (Norfolk). Here celestial symbolism pertaining to Roman, Celtic and oriental religion is present. Amongst other ritual material, including ceremonial staves (fig. 15) and bronze ravens, is the hollow-cast bronze head of the Roman Jupiter associated with a mask depicting the Graeco-Egyptian Heliosarapis (fig. 8) and a Celtic miniature wheel symbol (fig. 16).

Fig. 15 *(left)*. Bronze tip of ceremonial stave with attached rings possibly for the suspension of bells, from a religious hoard; Felmingham Hall, Norfolk. (Illustrator: P. J. Lopeman; copyright: Miranda Green.)
Fig. 16 *(right)*. Bronze wheel model, from religious hoard; Felmingham Hall, Norfolk. (Illustrator: P. J. Lopeman; copyright: Miranda Green.)

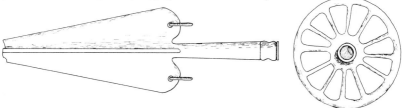
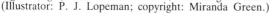

5
The Celtic gods

It is sometimes difficult to distinguish between Romano-Celtic divinities (those displaying both Roman and Celtic influence) and deities who are entirely Celtic in concept. The problems arise because even gods who are totally alien to the classical pantheon owe something to classical influence in the fact of representation and, sometimes, in their endowment with epigraphically recorded names. The gods studied in this chapter are those to whom direct counterparts cannot be found in the Graeco-Roman world and who, as divine concepts, are essentially foreign to Roman expressions of belief. Some Celtic gods are very localised even within Britain; others are known throughout Celtic Europe.

Mother-goddesses

A great many Celtic divinities have overt and very definite associations with fertility. This is natural and understandable in a society which was essentially rural and possessed an agricultural, pastoral and non-industrial economy. This divine fertility element is most obviously seen in the various 'mother-goddesses'. These take several forms, the most important being the *Deae Matres* (plate 35), who occur in triplicate, and representations of single seated females (plate 36). Both types are distinguished by being depictions of women either nursing infants or holding baskets of fruit, loaves or other fertility symbols such as fish.

The *Deae Matres* as a specific type occur both on dedications and as stone sculptures normally in triplicate, though a group of four has been discovered in London. The Mothers are present in a number of distinct areas in Britain, with outliers elsewhere. Places where they are particularly common include the Cotswolds and neighbouring areas, notably Cirencester (plate 35) and Bath, and also the region of Hadrian's Wall, Lincolnshire and London. Apart from London, where a silver plaque dedicated to the goddesses is also recorded, the distribution correlates with areas of good-quality stone. Sculptures of single Mothers are not common in Britain, but a stone example comes from Caerwent; a bronze figurine of a Mother nursing two infants is recorded from Culver Hole Cave on the Gower peninsula. Apart from their main fertility role, there is evidence that mother-goddesses have connections with water and with healing springs. At Bath

Plate 35. Relief of the *Deae Matres;* the seated goddesses bear fruit and loaves in their laps; Cirencester, Gloucestershire. (Photograph: C. J. Bowler; copyright: Corinium Museum.)

dedications occur to the *Suleviae*, known also at Cirencester, Colchester and in Gaul. The word is linked to the name 'Sulis', the Celtic healing divinity of Bath and, indeed, a very stylised schist plaque of the Three Mothers is recorded also from the town.

Apart from stone (and occasional bronze) depictions of Mothers, a large and homogeneous group of pipeclay figurines is recorded. In the context of mother-goddesses, two main types are of interest; one has been named by scholars the *Dea Nutrix* (nursing goddess) and resembles Juno Lucina (classical goddess of childbirth) (plate 36). The goddess is portrayed as a youngish woman seated in a high-backed wicker chair nursing one or two infants. Pipeclay figures of this type were made in factories in central Gaul and the Rhineland and exported only within Celtic lands to a Romano-Celtic clientele. In Britain they occur in sepulchral and domestic contexts. The *Dea Nutrix* does not occur as a Graeco-Roman religious figurine and it is probable that a Celtic Mother, similar to the stone examples, is here being represented. Unlike the stone carvings, the clay *Deae Nutrices* were personal objects of devotion, perhaps owned by women, propitiated in pregnancy and childbirth and buried with the dead as a protecting divinity. Apparently similar in purpose, though entirely different in form, is the so-called 'Pseudo-Venus', a type of pipeclay statuette which resembles the classical Venus (plate 24). It is suggested, however, that these figures are also images connected with a domestic fertility cult rather than that of the classical Venus, who is not otherwise particularly popular in the Celtic world. The context of the 'Venus' type seems to suggest a

Plate 36. Headless pipeclay figurines of *Deae Nutrices;* each goddess nurses two infants and is seated in a wicker chair; London. (Photograph and copyright: Museum of London.)

Plate 37. Bronze figurine of Epona seated between two foals; the group is mounted on a thin, perforated baseplate; the goddess bears a yoke against her left shoulder, and ears of corn rest in her lap; Wiltshire. (Photograph and copyright: British Museum.)

similar domestic, protective function to that of the *Dea Nutrix*. It occurs in shrines and graves as well as in secular domestic contexts, and, in Gaul especially, the figurines are frequently associated with healing sanctuaries and water. In Britain this link appears for instance at the therapeutic shrine of Springhead (Kent) and Bath, and possibly also in the Walbrook valley, London.

Epona

The Celtic horse-goddess, Epona, is very rarely depicted in Britain and, on the few occasions when she does occur, she is clearly far removed from her main Gaulish distribution centres. Her worship was most popular in eastern Gaul and the German *limes* (frontier). Epona (whose Celtic name implies specific association with horses) never appears separate from her equine companions. She is portrayed seated astride or side-saddle on a horse or between two ponies or foals. The emblems associated

Plate 38. Relief of three *genii cucullati,* with a seated mother-goddess; Daglingworth, Gloucestershire. (Photograph: C. J. Bowler; copyright: Corinium Museum.)

with the goddess in Britain and Gaul (for instance *paterae* and ears of corn) link the cult with fertility and prosperity, but she sometimes appears with a dog or a key, which may suggest additional underworld functions. The most interesting and complete British object pertaining to Epona's cult is a small bronze figurine from Wiltshire depicting the goddess seated between two ponies (plate 37). Lying in Epona's lap and on a *patera* held in her right hand are huge ears of corn; on her left arm the goddess bears a yoke.

Genii cucullati

These curious representations of hooded dwarves generally occur in triplicate. They wear the Gaulish hooded cloak or *cucullus* and on certain continental inscriptions are named *genii cucullati*. They are common in Gaul, Germany and in Britain, where they have a distribution pattern virtually identical to that of the *Deae Matres*, that is the West Country (especially the Cirencester area) (plates 38, 39) and the north. Whilst the artistic treatment of these figures is generally rudimentary, one of the

Plate 39. Relief of *genii cucullati*, portrayed as triangular, schematised figures; Cirencester, Gloucestershire. (Photograph: C. J. Bowler; copyright: Corinium Museum.)

Plate 40. Clay triple-vase on hollow ring-base. These curious vessels may have been associated with the worship of triads of deities; Chester. (Photograph and copyright: Grosvenor Museum, Chester.)

Cirencester carvings (plate 39) is noteworthy in reaching a high degree of schematism. Context and associations seem to link these godlings with prosperity, well-being and fertility. They are represented accompanying mother-goddesses in Gloucestershire (plate 38) and in the same region some of them carry eggs. At Springhead (Kent) and Bath their presence connects the cult with therapeutic spring ceremonies. Single *cucullati* occur occasionally in Britain but, as with the Mothers, triplication appears to be significant, and for the Celts the number three would appear to have possessed magical — perhaps apotropaic — importance (plate 40; see also plate 29).

Sucellus, Nodens and other divinities with Celtic names

Roman deities sometimes adopt Celtic epithets or surnames which are frequently descriptive or topographical. Where a Celtic name occurs alone it is sometimes difficult to establish whether the Roman name has been left out or whether the Celtic deity named on the inscription exists in his own right. A rule of thumb which, though somewhat arbitrary, may be valid is that a Celtic name denotes an independent god either if the name occurs linked with more than one Roman name, e.g. Mars Cocidius, Silvanus Cocidius, but sometimes occurs alone, e.g. *deus* Cocidius (see plate 16), or if the Celtic name always occurs alone.

A number of divine beings with Celtic names appear in Britain and must, as entities, have existed prior to the Roman period. Several, for example Abandinus at Godmanchester (Cambridgeshire), only occur once or twice in the whole Celtic world and we can have little idea as to who they were and what religious concepts they represented; one presumes local, protective deities. It is worthwhile to study two deities with Celtic names, one of whom, Sucellus, is recorded throughout western Europe and moreover, although named on one or two inscriptions, is identifiable mainly by physical type; the other, Nodens, is a purely British god.

Sucellus (the Good Striker) is a Celtic hammer-god; he is characterised by his appearance as a mature bearded male with, as his main (and identifying) emblem, a long-shafted hammer. He frequently occurs in company with a consort, named Nantosuelta (Winding River), who often carries a house model on a long pole; on the continent, where the couple appear most commonly, they are often accompanied by other attributes including ravens, dogs, barrels and pots. Once again, prosperity, beneficence and domesticity are implied by some of the attributes; the hammer itself is more obscure but it could represent thunder and thence rain and fertility. In Britain Sucellus is rare and he must be

Fig. 17 *(below)*. Silver finger-ring dedicated to the Gaulish hammer-god Sucellus; York. (Illustrator and copyright: Miranda Green.)
Fig. 18 *(right)*. Sheet-bronze sceptre-binding decorated in repoussé with crude Celtic sketches of divinities and mythological items, including a rudimentary figure of Sucellus with long-shafted hammer. When found, the strip was curled into a spiral as if having bound a wooden stave; Farley Heath Romano-Celtic temple, Surrey. (Illustrator and copyright: Miranda Green.)

Plate 41. Bronze eagle figurine; Woodeaton temple, Oxfordshire. (Photograph: Mrs B. Naggar; copyright: Ashmolean Museum, Oxford.)

regarded as a Gaulish import. The god is named on an octagonal silver ring at York (fig. 17) and appears on a relief accompanied by his consort at Thorpe in Nottinghamshire. Two other, more ambiguous items which may represent the god are a very crude relief from Chedworth (Gloucestershire) and the depiction from Farley Heath temple (Surrey) of a crude 'matchstick' figure with long-hafted hammer on a sheet-bronze sceptre binding displaying complex, if sketchily depicted, iconography in the form of punched decoration (fig. 18).

Nodens or Nodons is different from Sucellus in being wholly British and in never being represented in human form. Nodens is represented epigraphically at Cockersand Moss (Lancashire), where his name is linked with that of Mars, but his main sanctuary was a large temple complex at Lydney (Gloucestershire), a therapeutic site containing a number of buildings including a dormitory. Here Nodens is mentioned on inscriptions and is equated with both Mars and Silvanus, but also appears alone. Though no human image of the deity exists, a striking feature is the occurrence of no less than nine dog representations; here the dog may portray Nodens in animal form or may merely

be an attendant. Many of the finds (for instance the oculists'
stamps) attest the healing nature of the site, and it is thus
important to recall that in classical religion the dog is the
companion of the healer Aesculapius.

Divine beasts and zoomorphic monsters

Discussion of Nodens and Lydney leads naturally to a
consideration of divine animals in Celtic religion. Whilst beasts in
Graeco-Roman symbolism play an important ancillary role as
attendants, e.g. Venus' dove, Jupiter's eagle (plate 41), animals
in Celtic religion sometimes appear to possess primary importance. We have already seen instances of this with Epona (plate
37) and Nodens. In Britain, as in Gaul, the horse, bull, boar and
dog occur consistently either alone or with a number of different
divinities. Besides their constant appearance with Epona, horses
occur alone as figurines, for instance at Canterbury, and we have
seen that an equine Mars had a localised cult in eastern Britain
(plate 30). At Wroxeter in north-western Britain, too, a
fragmentary statue of a life-size stone horse may denote a horse
cult. Bulls and boars occur commonly as small bronzes: the
immediately pre-Roman bull and boar from Lexden (plates 1, 2)
have already been noted in chapter 1. A plaque of a slain boar
comes from the circular Roman temple at Muntham Court (West
Sussex) (plate 42), implying a hunting cult, but this same shrine
was associated also with a 200 foot (60 m) shaft containing
numerous dog skeletons. In the absence of direct evidence, one
may only guess at the interpretation of cults associated with
divine beasts. Horses were highly respected animals among Celtic
peoples and the creature may have been revered on account of its
secular value. There is some evidence from Celtic coins, and
continental data, that the horse also possesses a solar aspect.
Bulls and boars may be images of strength, ferocity and
indomitability — all qualities admired in a heroic Celtic society.

Two beast types are curious in that they both betray unnatural
characteristics. Both are Gaulish but appear occasionally in
British contexts. The first is the triple-horned bull, an otherwise
normal bull depiction but with the addition of a third horn.
British examples include a pipeclay figurine from a child's grave
at Colchester (plate 43), a three-horned bull's head forming part
of the mace-head from Willingham Fen (plate 32), and a silvered
bronze beast with the remains of human figures on its back from
the late shrine at Maiden Castle (plate 44). The addition of a third
horn is particularly interesting since once again the significance of

Plate 42. Bronze plaque of slain boar; the figure displays a balanced mixture of naturalism and schematism; Muntham Court Roman temple site, near Worthing, West Sussex. (Photograph and copyright: Worthing Museum and Art Gallery.)

Plate 43. Pipeclay triple-horned bull, from a child's grave; Colchester, Essex. (Photograph and copyright: Colchester and Essex Museum.)

Plate 44. Silver-washed bronze figurine of a triple-horned bull with busts of anthropomorphic deities on its back; late Romano-Celtic temple, Maiden Castle, Dorset. (Photograph
and copyright: Dorset County Museum.)

Plate 45. Relief of Cernunnos with two ram-horned snakes; Cirencester, Gloucestershire. (Photograph: C. J. Bowler; copyright: Corinium Museum.)

the number three is apparent. The second monstrous beast is the ram-horned snake. Again the concentration of objects depicting this creature is in eastern Gaul and there is only a scattering of portrayals from Britain. The combination, on one representation, of ram horns and snake is curious. In the Graeco-Roman world the serpent combines a death/earth and beneficent role; the ram was revered as a symbol of fertility and appears thus in its association with the classical Mercury. But the composite ram/snake concept is alien to the classical world, and one must assume deliberate Celtic compression of at least two ideas in one mythical beast. In Britain the ram-horned snake appears in company with the stag-horned god Cernunnos (see below) at Cirencester (plate 45), twined around a small altar at Lypiatt (Gloucestershire) (plate 46), and associated with a Celtic-looking

Plate 46. *(left).* Altar with ram-horned snake in relief twined around outside surface; Lypiatt Park, Gloucestershire. (Photograph and copyright: Stroud District Museum.)
Plate 47. *(right).* Stone severed head from shrine; Caerwent, Gwent. (Photograph and copyright: National Museum of Wales, Cardiff.)

Mars from a hoard of religious bronzes found in a pit at Southbroom (Wiltshire).

Horns and heads

Celtic gods in Britain are frequently anonymous. Often a being may be represented with neither emblem nor feature to identify its function, nor with any associated inscription giving its name. Many representations of such amorphous deities exist in British contexts and little may be said about them. However, two features of anthropomorphic Celtic images are particularly striking and deserve some mention. One is the phenomenon of representing gods with horns; the other is that of depicting deities merely by the head alone. Horned beings fall into two categories; one, a stag-antlered, usually cross-legged god we may identify as

Gaulish. On a Paris inscription he is called Cernunnos (Horned One) — a tautologous and uninformative title. Depictions of this type form a homogeneous group and it is clear that a specific god is represented. Cernunnos occurs rarely in Britain, but a Cirencester stone relief depicts the god accompanied by two ram-horned snakes, constant companions of this deity (plate 45). Antlers, ram-horned serpents and other attributes present on continental reliefs imply that a god of prosperity and well-being is being worshipped. The second type of horned depiction is, by contrast, more common in Britain than anywhere else in the Celtic world, especially in the north of the province (fig. 19). The type takes the form of the addition of horns (usually bull horns) to certain divinities, generally (but not always, fig. 20) portrayed in stone. Sometimes these horned gods bear other features identifying them with, for example, warrior-gods; but the vast majority possess no distinctive symbols.

Fig. 19 *(left)*. Stone bust of horned god; Moresby, Cumbria. (Illustrator: P. J. Lopeman; copyright: Miranda Green.)
Fig. 20 *(above)*. Bronze mask of bull-horned anthropomorphic deity; Athelney, Somerset. (Illustrator: P. J. Lopeman; copyright: Miranda Green.)

The presence of horned beings has links with another major type of representation, that of heads on their own (plate 47) (since horned gods are also often depicted only by the head). It is probable that so-called 'severed heads' merely represent Celtic deities whose identities are unknown to us, the head being considered the most important part to portray. Divine images in the most Celtic style sometimes appear as totally anonymous beings. British stone-carved heads such as that from Caerwent (plate 47) mean little to us, but such images must have held profound religious significance for the Celtic devotees who carved them or commissioned their production. Face-pots occur all over Britain and the continent and are probably part of the same kind of ritual expression (plate 48).

Plate 48. Pottery face-urn with bearded face; Caerwent, Gwent. (Photograph and copyright: National Museum of Wales, Cardiff.)

6
Christianity

Literary evidence

It is probable that Britons were unaware of Christ before the later second century AD. Classical writers of the third century AD such as Origen and Tertullian speak of British Christians, and by the early fourth century, when Constantine had established Christianity as the Roman state cult, we know that there were British bishops. At the Council of Arles in AD 314 there were three prelates from London, York and another town (possibly Lincoln, Caerleon or Colchester). From the mid fourth century onwards there is increasing evidence for the prominent role played by Christian communities and priests in Britain, both within the context of the orthodox church and in disputes and heresies, like that of Pelagianism (Pelagius was a monk from Britain).

The evidence for churches in the Roman period

Most data concerning churches in Roman Britain are inconclusive and rest both on literary allusion and on deductions from the presence of later buildings. One of the strongest candidates for a church within a major settlement is at Richborough (Kent), where foundation blocks for a timber church are suggested. The best attested town example is at Silchester (Hampshire), where a building with rectangular nave, side-aisles and an eastern narthex (entrance) and a small western apse is recorded; there is tenuous evidence for a fourth-century construction. A small basilican building of similar type is recorded at St Albans. This is of interest since we know from written sources that Albanus was martyred here either under the Emperor Geta (AD 209) or later under Diocletian. A *martyrium* (a shrine erected to commemorate a martyr) was probably constructed just outside the town, where Christian burials are attested.

Apart from urban and formal churches, we have evidence for 'estate' churches or rural, private churches within Roman villas. The most celebrated of these is at Lullingstone (Kent), a rich villa-estate. In the mid fourth century AD a suite of rooms at the northern end was blocked off internally but with its own external access. Two rooms bear Christian wall-paintings (fig. 21), motifs including the chi-rho monogram, the alpha and omega and human figures in attitudes of prayer. Two other villas evidence private Christian cult practices. Both are in Dorset; the house at Frampton contains a room with a mosaic decorated with an encircled chi-rho; the other, at Hinton St Mary, possesses a mosaic depicting a male head (generally interpreted as that of Christ himself) with a chi-rho behind.

Fig. 21. Reconstruction of wall-plaster showing Christian painting. The chi-rho monogram is encircled by a wreath; the birds may represent human souls; Lullingstone Roman villa, Kent. (Illustrator and copyright: Miranda Green.)

Christian hoards of metalwork

A phenomenon of the Roman evidence for Christianity in Britain is the burial of large amounts of silverware decorated with Christian symbolism. The Mildenhall Treasure is one such hoard, a silver table service whose pieces are marked with Christian motifs, but this cache should not be counted as evidence for Romano-British Christianity since the treasure was probably imported as the personal property of the Christian general Lupicinus, a master of horse in Gaul, sent to Britain with a field force in the year AD 360.

The most important treasure is the gold and silver hoard found at Water Newton (Cambridgeshire) in 1975 (plate 49). Its significance lies in the strong possibility that the cache was the communal property of an *ecclesia* or Christian group, and in the fact of its being the earliest hoard of its kind so far discovered. The findspot was probably within the boundaries of the Roman town of *Durobrivae*. The hoard consists of twenty-eight objects, one of which is gold; of these there are eight vessels (some inscribed), a wine strainer and eighteen plaques. One plaque is a sheet-gold appliqué disc, and some of them bear a gilt chi-rho.

Plate 49. Part of the Water Newton Christian silver treasure, showing three vessels, three plaques and a wine strainer; *Durobrivae*, Cambridgeshire. (Photograph and copyright: British Museum.)

The hoard contains fifteen examples of the Constantinian form of the chi-rho; one inscribed cup bears testimony to the presence of a sanctuary or church. The objects in this hoard were probably not abandoned; their discovery, obviously buried as one entity, suggests that recovery was intended. The cache could have been hidden for a number of reasons — against damage from members of a rival cult, theft, looting or political persecution. The most likely burial date was the earlier fourth century AD. The plate may well have been used by a community of practising Christians perhaps for sacramental purposes. Of special interest are the leaf- or feather-shaped plaques since they are of essentially pagan type of the kind hung up on the doors or walls of Romano-Celtic temples (like that of Uley, Gloucestershire). It is suggested that new Christian believers were encouraged to bring offerings already familiar to them in pagan worship.

Water Newton is not the only buried hoard of valuable tableware known from Britain. Others include that from Appleshaw (Hampshire), where one of thirty-two pewter vessels bears a chi-rho. All come from a metre-deep pit cut into the cement floor of a villa probably abandoned in the later fourth century. Biddulph (Staffordshire) has produced a small hoard of silver spoons, one of which bears a chi-rho; similar spoons are recorded from Dorchester (Dorset). All such caches possess the

common factor of belonging to wealthy families in settled
homesteads, and of being hidden away, for whatever reason,
during periods of unease in the fourth century AD.

Other evidence for Christianity

Christian objects are widely scattered over Britain and are of
great variety, ranging from constructional material evidencing
buildings to small, personal possessions. Such items include the
small sandstone block from Catterick (North Yorkshire), reused
in a bath-house, incised with a crude chi-rho; the slabs around the
spring and *nymphaeum* at Chedworth and the tile from York and
the brick from Leicester all show evidence for the Christianity of
building workers or owners. Complete vessels, like the pewter
bowls from London, Caerwent and Welney (Cambridgeshire),
the pottery lamp from Margate, and the late orange-ware bowl
from Richborough, may have been used in private sacramental
ceremonies. Potsherds marked with the chi-rho from, for
example, Canterbury and Exeter may once have belonged to
complete vessels and would have been similarly used. Large lead
tanks, such as that from Icklingham (Suffolk) (fig. 22) were
probably used in baptism.

Of small, valuable items, the most important group consists of
gold and silver finger-rings. These occur throughout the province;
an example from Brancaster (Norfolk) bears the Christian legend
vivas in Deo ('may you live in God'). The same inscription is
present on a ring from Silchester, an object which possesses the
added interest of mentioning a certain Senicianus, possibly the
same individual recorded as having stolen a ring from one
Silvanus who invoked the god Nodens on a lead curse at Lydney
against the thief.

In terms of distribution, the heaviest concentration of Christian
finds is undoubtedly in south-eastern Britain, the region subjected to the most prolonged and successful romanisation. From
this centre, one arm stretches west to Dorset, Gloucestershire
and south-east Wales; the other travels north along the eastern
side of Britain.

The evidence for Christianity in the Roman province of Britain
is thus scattered but enough survives in the form of structures,
rich metalwork and small objects to demonstrate archaeologically
that the cult gained a substantial foothold in Britain during the
fourth century. What were the reasons for its apparently early
success? Pagan oriental mystery cults and Christianity possessed
in common the appearance of exclusivity — of the creation of a

Fig. 22. Lead tank bearing the Christian symbols of the chi-rho and alpha and omega (first and last letters of the Greek alphabet, symbolising the beginning and the end). The tank may have been a baptismal font; Icklingham, Suffolk. (Illustrator: P. J. Lopeman; copyright: Miranda Green.)

distance between devotees and non-believers. The difference between the pagan eastern cults and Christianity was that the latter gave real hope to a people frequently oppressed, in later Roman Britain, by poverty and taxation. Christianity offered to everyone, regardless of wealth, social position or sex, a promise of salvation on acceptance of and commitment to the new faith.

Christianity: the end of paganism?

The official adoption of Christianity by Rome and the provinces after the Edict of Milan in AD 313 did not mean that British paganism immediately disappeared. On the contrary, there is some evidence of renewed pagan activity during the fourth century. An inscription from Cirencester set up by a governor of *Britannia Prima* attests to the restoration of a column and statue to Jupiter 'in honour of the Old Religion'. This must have taken place after the Diocletianic reorganisation of Britain in AD 296 into four provinces (one of which was *Prima*). The action could well have occurred during the time of the apostasy of the Emperor Julian in the 360s AD. Certain pagan temples were built in the fourth century and others were refurbished. A shrine of Romano-Celtic type was built at Maiden Castle after AD 367; another at Brean Down was erected in about 340. Lydney, though now thought to have been constructed originally in the later third or early fourth century, shows evidence of later fourth-century refurbishing. On the question of pagan survival, one or two other points may be made. There may have been political or religious reasons leading to the hiding away of

Christian silver plate during the fourth century. Witchcraft too may be evidenced by the decapitated skeletons from Hertfordshire which date from this time, like that from Sawbridgeworth. Finally, the resistance of paganism to Christianity is demonstrated by the literary evidence of Nennius, who records that in the mid fifth century Vortigern consulted not *episcopi* (bishops) but *magi* (magicians).

7
Museums

The following museums possess good collections of religious material of the Roman period, much of which is on display.

Ashmolean Museum of Art and Archaeology, Beaumont Street, Oxford OX1 2PH. Telephone: Oxford (0865) 512651.

Cambridge University Museum of Archaeology and Anthropology, Downing Street, Cambridge CB2 3DZ. Telephone: Cambridge (0223) 59714.

Carlisle Museum and Art Gallery, Castle Street, Carlisle, Cumbria CA3 8TP. Telephone: Carlisle (0228) 34781.

City of Bristol Museum and Art Gallery, Queens Road, Bristol BS8 1RL. Telephone: Bristol (0272) 299771.

Corinium Museum, Park Street, Cirencester, Gloucestershire GL7 2BX. Telephone: Cirencester (0285) 5611.

Gloucester City Museum and Art Gallery, Brunswick Road, Gloucester GL1 1HP. Telephone: Gloucester (0452) 24131.

Grosvenor Museum, 27 Grosvenor Street, Chester CH1 2DD. Telephone: Chester (0244) 21616 or 313858.

Museum of Antiquities of the University and the Society of Antiquaries of Newcastle upon Tyne, Department of Archaeology, The University, Newcastle upon Tyne NE1 7RU. Telephone: Newcastle upon Tyne (0632) 328511.

Museum of London, London Wall, London EC2Y 5HN. Telephone: 01-600 3699.

National Museum of Wales, Cathays Park, Cardiff CF1 3NP. Telephone: Cardiff (0222) 397951.

Roman Baths Museum, Pump Room, Stall Street, Bath, Avon BA1 1LZ. Telephone: Bath (0225) 61111.

Stroud District Museum, Lansdown, Stroud, Gloucestershire GL5 1BB. Telephone: Stroud (045 36) 3394.

8
Select bibliography

Ferguson, J. *The Religions of the Roman Empire*. Thames and Hudson, 1970.

Green, M. J. *A Corpus of Religious Material from the Civilian Areas of Roman Britain*. British Archaeological Reports, Oxford, number 24, 1976.

Green, M. J. *A Corpus of Small Cult Objects from Military Areas of Roman Britain*. British Archaeological Reports, Oxford, number 52, 1978.

Green, M. J. 'The Worship of the Romano-Celtic Wheel-God in Britain seen in relation to Gaulish Evidence', *Collections Latomus*, volume 38, fasc. 2 (1979), 345-68.

Harris, E. and J. *The Oriental Cults in Roman Britain*. E. J. Brill, 1963.

Lewis, M. J. T. *Temples in Roman Britain*. Cambridge, 1966.

Megaw, J. V. S. *Art of the European Iron Age*. Harper and Row, 1970.

Munby, J. and Henig, M. (editors). *Roman Life and Art in Britain*. British Archaeological Reports, Oxford, number 41, 1977.

Ogilvie, R. M. *The Romans and their Gods*. BCA, London, 1969.

Painter, K. S. *The Water Newton Early Christian Silver*. British Museum Publications Ltd, 1977.

Piggott, S. *The Druids*. Thames and Hudson, 1968.

Rodwell, W. (editor). *Temples, Churches and Religion in Roman Britain*. British Archaeological Reports, Oxford, number 77, 1980.

Ross, A. *Pagan Celtic Britain*. Routledge and Kegan Paul, 1967.

Thévenot, E. *Divinités et sanctuaires de la Gaule*. Fayard, 1968.

Thomas, C. *Christianity in Roman Britain*. Batsford, 1981.

Toynbee, J. M. C. *Art in Roman Britain*. Phaidon, 1962.

Toynbee, J. M. C. *Art in Britain under the Romans*. Oxford University Press, 1964.

Toynbee, J. M. C. *Animals in Roman Life and Art*. Thames and Hudson, 1973.

Vries, J. de. *La Religion des Celtes*. Paris, 1963.

Wedlake, W. J. *The Excavation of the Shrine of Apollo at Nettleton, Wiltshire, 1956-1971*. Society of Antiquaries of London/Thames and Hudson, 1982.

9
Glossary

Anthropomorphic: having the form of a human being.

Apotropaic: possessing the power to avert evil.

Caduceus: herald's staff, wand of Mercury; the object generally consists of a winged staff with entwined serpents.

Chi-rho: the first two letters of the word 'Christ' in Greek.

Chthonic: from Greek *chthonos* (earth); pertaining to the underworld.

Cyclical: pertaining to mythology based on the year's seasonal cycle.

Dualism: in religion, two opposed and opposite but inter-dependent elements, usually good and evil, light and darkness, life and death.

Epigraphy: collective term for inscriptions, usually on stone.

Escutcheon: shield-shaped bucket handle-mounting with ring handle.

Iconography: collective term for figural images on stone, bronze and other materials.

Nymphaeum: shrine dedicated to water spirits, incorporating a pool.

Porphyry: an igneous rock having a purplish base with embedded quartz crystals; in ancient times quarried in Egypt.

Repoussé: the main method of producing relief decoration on silver and bronze. The metal is placed on a bed of soft pitch (which both supports the metal and yields); a hammer and punch are then used to push out the decorative pattern.

Triad: collection of three deities, usually linked in some way.

Verism: description of art which is naturalistic, a faithful copy of reality or of life.

Index

Abandinus 58
Aesculapius 38, 60
Ahriman 17, 20
Alde, river 28, 29
Apis 26
Apollo 37, 39
Apollo Cunomaglus 43
Appleshaw 69
Astarte 26
Atargatis 18, 26
Athelney 65
Atys 20, 22, 23
Bacchus 18, 38, 48
Ballachulish 6, 8
Bancroft 34
Barkway 31, 32
Bath 30, 31, 37, 41, 43, 44, 51, 52, 54, 57
Belatucadrus 44
Benwell 31
Bes 26
Bewcastle 33
Biddulph 69
Birdoswald 31, 37, 39, 49
Bisley 30, 45
Boar 8, 9, 10, 60, 61
Brancaster 70
Brean Down 71
Brigstock 45
Bull 8, 9, 10, 18, 20, 60, 65
Bury St Edmunds 31
Caerleon 49, 50, 67
Caerwent 16, 20, 26, 44, 51, 64, 66, 70
Caesar 13
Canterbury 30, 60, 70
Carlisle 36, 38
Carrawburgh 17
Castlesteads 49
Catterick 70
Ceres 38, 39
Cernunnos 63, 65
Charlton Down 30
Chedworth 59, 70
Chester 30, 57
Chesters 43
Chiddingfold 26
Christianity 67, 68, 69, 70, 71, 72
Cirencester 26, 34, 48, 51, 52, 56, 57, 63, 65, 71
Cocidius 33, 44, 58. See also *Mars.*
Cockerel 15, 33, 34, 35
Cockersand Moss 59
Colchester 8, 9, 29, 37, 43, 52, 60, 61, 67
Corbridge 22, 23, 26, 30, 50
Crewelthorpe 39
Crows 8, 58
Culver Hole Cave 51

Cupid 38
Curses 35, 43
Custom Scrubs 45
Cybele 20, 22, 23
Dagenham 6, 8
Daglingworth 55
Dea Nutrix 52, 53, 54
Deposit, ritual 11
Diana 38, 41
Dioscuri 18
Discipulina 42
Dog 18, 25, 56, 58, 59, 60
Dolphin 49, 50
Dorchester, Dorset 25, 69
Druids 13
Duns Tew 35
Eagle 49, 50, 59, 60
Earith 31
Emberton 41, 43
Enclosure, ritual 8
Epona 54, 56, 60
Exeter 70
Face-pot 66
Farley Heath 26, 58, 59
Faunus 42
Felmingham Hall 25, 50
Flora 38
Fortuna 38, 41, 42
Foss Dyke 6, 31
Frampton 68
Frilford 11
Froxfield 23
Genius 25, 36, 37, 38, 49, 50
Genius cucullatus 55, 56, 57
Gloucester 20, 21, 22, 42
Goat 35
Godmanchester 58
Harpocrates 23, 25
Head 64, 66
Healing 38, 44, 51, 54, 57, 60
Heliosarapis 25, 26
Hercules 26, 37, 38
Highworth 25
Hinton St Mary 68
Hoard, sacred 32, 68, 69
Hockwold 23
Horns 9, 43, 60, 63, 64, 65, 66
Horse 54, 56, 60
Horseman 45, 47, 48, 60
Horus 23, 25, 26
Hounslow 8
Housesteads 17, 18, 21, 31
Hunter-god 37, 60. See also e.g. *Diana, Silvanus.*
Icklingham 70, 71
Imperial cult 6, 16, 20, 28, 29, 37

Isis 23, 24, 25
Juno 29, 38
Juno Lucina 52
Jupiter 29, 31, 46, 48, 49, 50, 71
Jupiter Ammon 26
Jupiter columns 46, 48, 50
Jupiter Dolichenus 26, 27
Leicester 70
Lincoln 29, 51, 67
Llyn Cerrig 11
London 11, 17, 18, 19, 20, 22, 23, 24, 25, 26, 27, 29, 30, 31, 34, 51, 53, 54, 67, 70
Lower Slaughter 46
Lucan 46
Lullingstone 67
Luna 18, 38
Lydney 59, 60, 70, 71
Lypiatt Park 30, 63, 64
Maiden Castle 38, 60, 62, 71
Margate 70
Mars (and Warriors) 6, 11, 15, 30, 31, 32, 33, 43, 44, 45, 46, 50, 59, 60, 64, 65
Mars Corotiacus 46
Mars Lenus Ocelus Vellaunus 16, 44
Mars Toutatis 32
Martlesham 45
Maryport 31
Mercury 15, 18, 31, 33, 34, 35, 41, 42, 43, 63
Mercury Andescocioucus 29
Milber Down 8, 10
Mildenhall 22, 23, 68
Minerva 18, 28, 29, 30, 31, 38, 43, 44
Miniature objects 11, 12, 13, 31, 50
Mithras 17, 18, 20, 21, 27
Moresby 65
Mother-goddess 51, 52, 53, 56, 57
Muntham Court 60, 61
Nantosuelta 58
Nemesis 42
Nennius 72
Neptune 38
Netherby 50
Nettleton Shrub 37, 38, 39, 43
Newtown 31
Nodens 57, 59, 60, 70
Orange 18
Origen 67
Osiris 23, 26
Paris 65
Peacock 30
Pelagius 67
Peterborough 45, 47
Pits 11, 37
Plaxtol 30
Priests 13, 29, 67
Ram 15, 34, 63
Richborough 67, 70
Rosmerta 42, 43

St Donats 33
Salus 42
Sarapis 18, 19, 23, 25
Sawbridgeworth 72
Sawtry 26, 27
Scorpion 17, 18
Segontium 17
Seneca 29
Silchester 25, 67, 70
Silvanus 37, 58, 59, 70
Silvanus Callirius 38, 43
Sky-god 43, 46, 48
Snake 17, 18, 25, 48, 63
Snake, ram-horned 63, 64, 65
Solar cults 8, 18, 20, 46, 48, 49, 50, 60
Sol Invictus 20, 26, 27
Southbroom 64
Springhead 54, 57
Stag 8, 37, 38, 63, 64
Stone, Bucks 25
Stony Stratford 31
Sucellus 57, 58, 59
Suleviae 52
Sulis 31, 43, 52
Tacitus 29
Tanarus 46
Tertullian 67
Thetford 42
Thornborough 25
Thorpe 59
Thoth 26
Tortoise 15, 25, 33, 34
Tree 48
Trier 44
Triple-horned bull 49, 50, 60, 61, 62
Triplism 45, 46, 56, 57
Uley 34, 35, 43, 69
Venus 38, 40, 41, 53
Verulamium 15, 33, 38, 67
Vesta 38
Victory 38, 41, 42
Vulcan 35, 37
Warrior. See *Mars.*
Water 11, 51, 54
Water-bird 8, 10
Water Newton 68
Well 46, 60
Welney 70
West Stoke 31
Wetwang Slack 6, 8
Whatley 23
Wheel 8, 48, 50
Willingham Fen 49, 50, 60
Witchcraft 72
Witham 8, 10
Woodeaton 12, 13, 15, 28, 31, 32, 59
Worth 11
Wroxeter 60
York 10, 29, 30, 58, 59, 67, 70